Out of Oblivion

Kenisha Kaushal

BookLeaf
Publishing

India | USA | UK

Presentation by *BookLeaf Publishing*

Web: www.bookleafpub.com

E-mail: info@bookleafpub.com

ISBN: 9789358739626

First edition 2023

DEDICATION

To those who inspired me to write.And to my mother,Your support is all I'll ever need.

PREFACE

About 6910 days ago, I was born in the holy city of Kurukshetra, where, according to the Hindu epic Mahabharata, the Mahabharata War took place and the sacred Bhagavad Gita was delivered as a sermon. Beyond its religious significance, the Mahabharata is the longest epic poem known to date and holds a crucial place in world literature. Thus, my birthplace itself may account for my passion for literature and poetry. Consequently, I've always been passionate about poetry, but as a shy young girl, I didn't have the courage to follow my calling and showcase my talent to the world. However, in solitude, I wrote ardently about everything that crossed my mind: all of my opinions that were not respected, all of the words a young, shy girl could not utter, and all of the art that an aspiring artist could not create. That was until I decided to step out of oblivion and pour my heart into this book.

This book is akin to an artist's first art exhibition. It is the voice of that shy, young girl. It is a doorway for you to step into my world and become a part of it. I hope that you find as much meaning and inspiration in these pages as I have in the act of writing them.

Out of Oblivion

I must get rid of this nothingness concealing my
creations,
Because I am not a committed crime that must
not be revealed.
I am not a prisoner of war, I am not a poem left
half-written.
I am the promise a little girl made to herself to
see this world,
To throw her forbidden mask, to open her big
bright brown eyes.
She must stop playing this prolonged game of
hide and seek.
No more unsent love letters in those secret spots,
No more judgments on my own body's
silhouette in the light.
I must get rid of this nothingness and step out of
oblivion.

Dear Old Me,

Dear Old Me,
They were all right: Loosen up a bit.
Don't think too much about your crooked smile
Or adjust your skirt while you sit.
Don't hesitate to experiment more with your
style.

Dear Old Me,
Your pimples will slowly fade away.
You'll show more teeth as your laugh gets less
fake.
Your body will gain weight, in a healthy way.
So, someday you won't hesitate to eat a little
more cake.

Dear Old Me,
The hard work doesn't really pay off like you
imagined.
But the heartache does shape you into a stronger
version.
The cooler older girls you secretly admire
happened
To be who you grow up to become as a person.

Dear Old Me,

The cold lonely nights will see a bright sunrise.
You'll make many friends who won't hurt you.
But friends go by like seasons, you'll realize.
Soon, their memories fade away too.

Dear Old Me,
I know what success means to you, my dear.
But I have experienced love, anger, joy- all by
now.
Just hold on tight, your happiness is so, so near.
Don't worry! Things always work out somehow.

I am

I am a Potter, for I often mould myself into a
vessel
To fill all the ecstasies in this huge universe
within me.
I fill myself with all of life's delicacies by
acquiring
Various shapes. Yet, nothing seems to truly
fulfill me.

I am a Farmer. I grow whatever helps me
Nourish my body, my mind, and my soul.
But I even demolish: I plant seedlings in the sun
Only to rip them off for my own hunger.

I am Writer, because I rewrote my own story,
And narrated it in a way I wanted it to be.
Manipulation, in the name of artistic license,
Is how I process my emotions in any life crisis.

Mi Amor

When will sugar stop tasting sweet?
How can we propagate world peace?
What if the ocean and sky somehow meet?
Why can't man get over his greed?

Why do stars only twinkle at night?
What makes your eyes shine so bright?
When will we ever end this fight
For there is no need to justify human rights?

How do people sleep in starvation?
Why can't we put an end to discrimination?
When could we afford free medication?
Will women ever really attain liberation?

Why don't childhood friends talk anymore?
How can history be synonymous to bore?
Tell me truthfully mi amor,
What is it that makes you want more?

I open my eyes

I open my eyes and find myself walking.
Barefoot, I wander around hopelessly.
The map is printed in a foreign language.
The compass needle won't stop flickering.
I find myself walking in the maze of mediocrity.

I open my eyes and trip over the foothill.
I gasp, I yell, I feel myself helplessly falling,
With no time to imagine the aftermath.
The survivor within me can't really be killed.
The winner in me can witness me failing.

I open my eyes and accelerate my car.
The thrill of the rush brings me back to life.
The adrenaline in my body is well justified.
But an instant waver in my built-in radar
Premonishes my crash and ends my drive.

A love letter to my loneliness

Never in my existence have I ever felt lonely
When I'm all alone. It hits me when I'm with
company:
Faking smiles for a false candid, and pretending
To understand inside jokes while cleverly
concealing
The void within me. It is like that codependent
lover
That sticks by my side even when the party's
over.

Till today

The discomfort I feel
In my own rose-tinted skin reminds me
Of how much I don't belong
To this city that always steals all of
My joys and stops me from being free,
From being me.

I wonder sometimes how long
Must I wait to admire
The life I wake up to everyday.
To feel confident and secure
In my own rose-tinted skin is a desire
I long for till this date,
Till today.

Tell Us About Yourself.

I see this gray world through a blurry frame
hiding my brown eyes.
I carry the load of my black hair, which I truly
detest,
But not more than the cellulite that is wrapped
around my thighs
Or the overconfidence I reflect through my
puffed chest.

I am not religious but I bow down to Him in
need.
I am opinionated but my voice is never heard.
I barely make enough money to buy every
finance book I can read.
I wish I owned a poet's pen or the wings of
birds.

I never forget birthdays, and I never remember
names.
My shelf is filled with slam books and stamps.
My favourite makeup is my birthday cake.
I inherited philately from gramps.

I wasn't raised at my birthplace.
I was not born flexible(had to stretch each and
every day).

I can touch my toes but I struggle to tie my lace
For kids never called me outdoors to play.

I am the gifted child, the youngster with
academic validation,
The good kid with a nasty side; thongs
underneath the man trouser.
I crave attention. I cry over a math equation.
My mind has 58 windows open, it's a web
browser.

I procrastinate, I work, I procrastinate again.
I consume 'less' caffeine in tea.
I believe that utter disappointment comes from
men.
For we are yet to be free, 'Let's Smash the
Patriarchy'.

Alpha male during the day, femme fatal by
night.
'Can't let him love me' because love can never
suffice.
Yet, I find myself trapped in daydreams, love
songs, and lip bites.
And think for a moment that having someone
would be nice.

I can't drive fast and my thoughts can't walk
slow.
I barf words out by my mouth at light speed.
I don't end relations that I outgrow.
My anxiety or me? Let's see who will succeed

I don't crochet

I don't crochet, not anymore.
I have spent many summers sitting
On the sofa, knitting out of bore.
But like my childhood, I've let it go.

I don't crochet anymore because
The sweater I started to knit didn't
Comfort me that night. It was
Woven to tie me tight in big fat lies

My Childhood

It seems like I stepped out of the womb as an
adult,
Burdened with life and its responsibilities.
I never colored out of the lines or broke a glass
window.
Too often, I ask myself where did my childhood
go?

The Protagonist

"Where have you been?
What do you smoke?
When did you lose all of your hope?
Why do you run like you're being chased?
How can people ever call you a disgrace?"

I've been through the driest of deserts
And the chilliest of mountains.
I've seen narrow lanes and a wide carriage.
I've smoked cigars, weed and drugs
Like lust and greed. For that guilty, I plead.
You can't lose what you never had:
Hope has never really consumed me.
I run fast enough to prove time is an illusion,
Pain is what my feet can't feel.
I run for money, for clarity, for passion,
For the heat. But mostly, I run for me.
People solely judge because of jealousy.
Man envies those that he wants to be.

I Stared in the Mirror And…

I stared in the mirror and saw her again,
The little toddler who loved dancing in the rain.
Her big bright eyes had seen no pain.
I waved at her and let her eternal joy remain.

I stared in the mirror and saw her afraid,
The most solemn stoic kid in the third grade.
Her toys were the only reason her friends
played.
I hugged her and told her bad times will fade.

I stared in the mirror and never thought who'd I
see,
Was the person who had long ago ruined me,
That's when I gave my ugly image a guarantee,
What I despise is not what I am fated to be

I have friends

I have friends, I've got many of them.
We will live, love, and laugh till the end of time.
But between all those jokes and silly smiles,
Each of them yearns for another company over
mine.

I have friends, but they don't understand
The life I narrate in tales isn't just in my head.
They don't understand we're not the same.
They often think my jokes are lame

I have friends, when I have toys to play.
They call me their best friend, what can I say!
But when the game is over at the end of the day,
I'm still that little girl hoping they'd stay.

Outgrew

When I see the dusky old faces of my childhood
friends,
I'm reminded not all good things come to an end,
Not everything that I adore is stolen from my
arms,
Not every happy dream ends with my morning
alarm.

When I look at those weary grown smiles of
theirs,
I recall my childhood's fun and forget my
worldly affairs.
Oh, the fun, the innocence, the jokes we
cracked,
And all those moments we'll never get back.

But when I look deeper into their eyes,
I try hard to forget their foolish and petty lies.
We still laugh together, just like we used to do,
It's tragic when you meet someone you outgrew.

How Do I Confess?

A subtle cheek pull and gentle hair flicks.
Capturing my laughter in the camera's clicks.
Waking up at 5 am, having pasta to cook.
Tracing their name all over my cracked foot.
Buying me the sweetest chocolates on bitter
days.
Letting me win every sport, each time we play.
Late night reading of poetry to help me sleep.
Stealing their shirts, novels,and hearts to keep.
Long stares across the room and forehead kisses.
Healing taught me to walk over burnt bridges.
Rearranging my dirty shoes and socks in a shoe
rack.
Teaching me everything that I mustn't lack.
Dancing together on stage in front of a million
eyes.
Reminiscing on how quickly time flies.
Sharing tales of the adventures of my childhood.
Them saying all the right things that they ever
could.
Fitting my shivering hand in one of their gloves.
How do I confess? I'm not used to this love.

Dream

What is art,
The coloured canvas or its artist's feeble fingers?
What is more graceful,
A ballerina's scarred feet or the pirouette she
leaps?
Is the book more tragic
Or the author's inspiration to write the tale?
What good is a dream until
The dreamer brings life into it, without fail?

Invisible

It seems the world turns deaf
As soon as I raise my voice.
My absence goes unnoticed.
My disappearance won't be
Acknowledged.
The words uttering from
My mouth seem like a bore.
Will I ever be interesting
Enough for you to adore?

My Body

When will I understand my body is not like the
dough
that I use to cook the food that I don't eat.
It's not a canvas put in an art gallery to be
adored by others.
It's not some gossip in a teenage girl's ears.
It's worth more than mere twenty-eight inches.
It's a museum of my past, and a muse for my
future.
It's a home for my mind. It's a home for my
soul.

Already

For every drop of water you spill on me,
I've already swallowed salty seas of it.
For every rose you pluck for me,
I've already spent several summers as a
sunflower.
For every love letter you write,
I've already been muse to poetry books.
For every second you spend with me,
I've already lived lifetimes of lonesome.

Together.

If we are trapped together, we must leave
together.
I see you from the keyhole working hard.
And eavesdrop on conversations I'm barred.
We play pretend and deny our problems,
But we know how our lives are marred.

If we are trapped together, we must leave
together.
I must stop relying on our good fair luck.
I don't blame you for keeping me stuck.
But this air seems to suffocate my lungs
And so a plan, within me, struck.

If we are trapped together, we must leave
together.
That's how it was supposed to be.
But, my dear, I can't bear any of this misery.
I must search for a way out.
The whole world awaits me.

www.ingramcontent.com/pod-product-compliance
Lightning Source LLC
LaVergne TN
LVHW051250200726
843510LV00011B/1780